WHEN I SEE YOU, I SEE ME

AuthorHouse™
1663 Liberty Drive
Bloomington, IN 47403
www.authorhouse.com
Phone: 833-262-8899

Because of the dynamic nature of the Internet, any web addresses or links contained in
this book may have changed since publication and may no longer be valid. The views
expressed in this work are solely those of the author and do not necessarily reflect the
views of the publisher, and the publisher hereby disclaims any responsibility for them.

This book is printed on acid-free paper.

ISBN: 978-1-6655-6993-4 (sc)
ISBN: 978-1-6655-6992-7 (e)

Library of Congress Control Number: 2022916315

Print information available on the last page.

Published by AuthorHouse 09/08/2022

authorHOUSE®

WHEN I SEE YOU, I SEE ME

MICHAEL T. SAVAGE
Illustrations by: Ricky L. Thomas

CONTENTS

PREFACE

This book is intended to introduce a rite of passage for African/black boys. Read this book as early and often to every African/black boy you can, their brain power is infinite. They will understand and comprehend.

As I stare at the mirror, I see my black skin shining in the light. This bold skin reflects with beauty and confidence. Every day I am aware of all the young black men that look at themselves, just as I do. It is crucial these young men know their value, their history and their power. This power that is depressed by our society at large; however, the evidence is so noticeable. All you must do is open your eyes and your mind.

PRESSURE

Black boys gracefully growing into black men. The process can be captivating and inspiring; to watch a young man's personality, develop along with characteristics and opinions. These events should be valued, knowing that the foundation of this development will have to uphold a significant amount of weight. Each young black boy inside this entire Universe is greatly valued. Regardless of one's situation or circumstance your contributions are important to the African/ black community.

When I see young black men, I see greatness, not potential, but greatness at the very moment. I am fully aware that some of the young men I see, are not aware of their own greatness and importance. It is up to all African/black women and men, young and old in our community to honor this greatness, embrace it and circulate it. This must be the mindset of our community. This mindset starts with you!

The pressure you will endure you are conditioned for. The power is in your DNA. The expectations of your greatness will shine through every situation in your life. You simply must remember who you are. The knowledge of self is a major key. The pressure of you being a black boy growing into a black man will provide a platform for you to shine with your mind, your skin, and your soul.

PLAN

Do you dream? I know when people ask you what you aspire to be in life; you think should you tell them your real dreams or just make up an answer to move the conversation forward. Maybe the question still wonders in your mind, not having an answer is okay, however; this answer must prioritize your thoughts. This answer will determine many things in your future.

This answer is up to you even if your parents are directing you in a certain workforce or career, if you have a clear plan and desire along with passion to do something, they will support you. If you have not started writing down goals for you to accomplish, today is the appropriate day. Goals, 5-year plan, 10- year plan, 20- year plan even a 50-year plan. To plan this far is not insane, the focus is based on clarity, having a plan will shape your mentality. Why not reach your highest potential?

Why not focus on planning to become the best version of yourself? What if God told you that you are a God? Would this change your thoughts and behavior? Would you rather believe, or would you rather know? As you dream or sleep at night see yourself being exactly where you want to be as an adult. What city, what career path, what business or things you want to own.

This vision will develop into real life. Having a clear direction of where you are going in life will present the map for you to reach your destination. All you must do is simply travel in that direction. How fast or slow you reach the destination depends solely on you. The most important part is to have a clear plan and have discipline in following through with your plan.

LEGACY

At some point the roles must switch in a man's life. You should go from your parents taking care of you to you positioning yourself to care for them. This requirement does not mean you have to provide for them financially in every aspect; yet, you are in a position of security that if you had to than you could. In your legacy, you must ensure it continues and the only way to do so is to plan and execute.

Being a true man, comes with responsibility. This responsibility is an honor not a burden. If your parents or parent, provides for you in the best manner they can you are responsible for making the best of your potential in order to take your legacy further and to make them proud of all your work.

This is a great honor and privilege to at some point assist in the lives of those who raised you, to ensure their happiness and well-being even if it is only by being the best person you can be.

The greatest honor you will ever have in life is being the son of your mother. That Goddess gave life to you. Honor that amazing gift by being the best man you can be.

Look for knowledge and apply it daily in your life. The legacy of your last name should mean everything to you and should be recognized and respected by everyone else. The legacy of your family should consist of truth and honesty with the goals and values that you believe in. A man provides and leads by example to uphold those values that he intends for his families last name to represent.

A man always does this, in every situation. Acknowledge the great men that lived and died before you in our culture. Allow their values and actions to inspire you in your own legacy.

The great African God you will become, you are today. Embrace your journey and pave your legacy. Everything you need is already inside of you.

Love,

From one African God to another African God.

Printed in the United States
by Baker & Taylor Publisher Services